LANDMARKS *of* FAITH

MARK L. GRAHAM

WestBow
PRESS®
A DIVISION OF THOMAS NELSON
& ZONDERVAN

WestBow Press books may be ordered through booksellers or by contacting:

WestBow Press
A Division of Thomas Nelson & Zondervan
1663 Liberty Drive
Bloomington, IN 47403
www.westbowpress.com
844-714-3454

Scripture taken from the King James Version of the Bible.

ISBN: 978-1-6642-7133-3 (sc)
ISBN: 978-1-6642-7134-0 (e)

Library of Congress Control Number: 2022912307

Print information available on the last page.

WestBow Press rev. date: 7/14/2022

ABOUT THE AUTHOR

Dr. Mark L. Graham holds A. A. and B.R.E. degrees from Baptist Bible College in Clarks Summit, Pennsylvania, as well as M.Div. and D. Min. degrees from Luther Rice Seminary in Jacksonville, Florida. He has also pursued study in the Greek Classics at Cornell University and trained at the Christian Counseling and Education Foundation of Laverock, Pennsylvania. Author of *Harnessing the Harassment of Human Fears*, Westbow Press, and several other counseling helps, Pastor Graham has an intense burden for the nurturing of New Testament churches. Having now served in local churches for nearly fifty years, as well as directing the Genesis Ministries (www.genesisministry.org) for twenty-five years, Dr. Graham is equipped to share biblical insight for the resolution of conflicts that God's people are facing today. Currently, Pastor Graham is pastor at Skyline Baptist Church of Rome, NY.

ACKNOWLEDGEMENTS

In sincere acknowledgement of and appreciation for the following co-laborers:

To my wife Diane, who, along with juggling the many responsibilities of our four children and those labors incumbent on a pastor's wife, made the time to edit her husband's writing attempts.

To all those at Immanuel Baptist Church who have helped in many ways to further God's Word through this publication.

To Carole Mack, whose secretarial skills contributed to the preparation and completion of this workbook.

To Vance Duncan and his daughter, Danielle, who have labored with me in the revision of this manual, thirty-two years from its original print. Vance's lucid advice and textual input, together with his daughter's critical preparation of this script, have provided unmeasured blessing to many lives through their devoted labors.

To my Savior Jesus Christ, the very dearest of friends, whose great love and patience toward me compel me to put forth my best effort for the sake of the kingdom!

All Scripture quotations in this publication are taken from the King James translation of the Bible.

CONTENTS

INSTRUCTIONS

The Psalmist refers to God's Word as more desirable than gold, "yea, than much fine gold" (Psa. 19:10). Since gold is so valuable, it is kept in a secure place and drawn upon as there is a need. The material in this book has been quarried from God's Word and is therefore precious! I would recommend the following to each reader: purchase your own notebook and keep your priceless finds in a secure place. Refer to your Landmarks as you sense the need. I would encourage you to fill in all the blanks by answering each question. Ask your Pastor or a trusted Christian friend to check over your answers once you have completed a particular session. May you find this study to be an enrichment to your Christian life and testimony!

THE BIBLE—GOD'S WORD

(BIBLIOLOGY)

I. Instruction: What the Bible teaches us about itself

  A. Inspired of God

    1. What type of men did God use to write the scriptures? (2 Pet. 1:21)

      _____.

    2. Who moved upon the personalities of human instruments to declare God's Word? (2 Pet. 1:21).

      _____.

    3. According to 2 Peter 1:20, the Word of God did not come to us by anyone's private

      _____.

    4. Whether we refer to history, geography, science, or other subjects of the Bible, Holy Scripture is said to be inspired in what aspects? (2 Tim. 3:16)

      _____.

  B. Preserved of God

    1. How long will the Word of God endure? (Psa. 119:89; Matt. 24:35; 1 Pet. 1:24–25)

      _____.

    2. Jesus taught that neither one jot nor tittle could pass from the law until two things passed away. What are these two things? (Matt. 5:18) _____ and _____.

  C. Interpreted of God

    1. What type of individual is not capable of comprehending the true sense of the Scriptures? (1 Cor. 2:14)

      _____.

2. First Corinthians 2:14 teaches us how the Bible is to be discerned. What is this important element?

    _____.

3. Although the Bible's teaching may have many applications, we are commanded to interpret it one way. What way are we encouraged to divide/interpret the Scripture? (2 Tim. 2:15)

    _____.

4. Whom did Jesus promise to send to believers, enabling them to understand the Bible? (John 16:13)

    _____.

5. What is the penalty for perverting the truth of God's Word, the Bible? (Rev. 22:18–19)

    _____.

II. Impact: The application of these truths in my life

   A. Because the Bible is God's Word, we are compelled to desire it more than what? (Psa. 19:10)

    _____.

   B. Because the Bible is God's Word, we are compelled to do what faithfully? (2 Tim. 2:15)

    _____.

   C. Because the Bible is God's Word, we are compelled to let its precepts dwell within us in what way? (Col. 3:16)

    _____.

   D. Why is it essential that we search the Scriptures? (John 5:39)

    _____.

   E. How will God's Word equip us for every good work and service? (2 Tim. 3:16–17)

    _____.

   F. The Word of God applied to our hearts will keep us from what? (Psa. 119:11)

    _____.

   G. The Word of God is able to rightly discern two things within the heart of a person. What are these two things? (Heb. 4:11) _____
       and _____.

   H. Jesus declared that in order for any person to be truly sustained in life, one needs more than bread. What else did the Lord say that people need? (Deut. 8:3; Matt. 4:4)

    _____.

GOD—OUR HEAVENLY FATHER
(THEOLOGY PROPER)

I. Instruction: What the Bible teaches us about God the Father

    A. God described in Scripture

        1. In John 4:24, God is said to be what? _____.

        2. In First John 1:5, God is said to be what? _____.

        3. In First John 4:16, God is said to be what? _____.

        4. In Hebrews 12:29, God is said to be what? _____.

    B. Leading characteristics of God

        1. What word does the Bible use to express God as all-powerful? (Rev. 19:6)

            _____.

        2. Psalm 139 describes the omniscience of God. What key word in this Psalm helps us understand and define this quality of God? (v. 6)

            _____.

        3. The omnipresence of God is evident from the fact that it is impossible for a person to flee from God's what? (Psa. 139:7)

            _____.

        4. The eternality of God is described in Psalm 90:2 as being from what to what?

            _____ to _____.

        5. The immutability of God is established by the fact that God cannot do what? (Mal. 3:6; Heb. 13:8)

            _____.

        6. The Bible describes what characteristic of God as His reigning quality? (Isa. 6:3; 1 Pet. 1:15–16; Rev. 4:8)

            _____.

7. God would have people know that the following characteristics are also true of Him. What are these communicative qualities?

_____ (Psa. 37:26).

_____ (Psa. 51:14).

_____ and _____ (Eph. 2:4).

_____ (Psa. 119:68).

_____ (2 Cor. 1:18).

8. Although God is one God, He is described as three coequal, coeternal Persons. Who are these three Persons of the Godhead?[1] (Matt. 28:19) The _____, the _____, and the _____.

9. Peter describes God as the faithful what? (2 Pet. 4:19) _____.

II. Impact: The application of these truths in my life

A. In what three aspects are we commanded to love the God of the Bible? (Deut. 6:5)
_____, _____, and _____.

B. What three things are the people of God bidden to do unto the Lord and in obedience to God? (Deut. 6:13) _____,
_____, and _____.

C. Because God is the Holy Sovereign, we are commanded not to use His name in what way? (Deut. 5:11)

_____.

D. The holiness of God requires what quality among His people? (1 Pet. 1:15–16)

_____.

E. What act of obedience is becoming to those who reverence God? (Psa. 22:3; Rev. 5:14)

_____.

F. What three elements characterize the people of God in Psalm 100:4?

_____, _____, and _____.

G. What does God desire in the inward parts of our lives? (Psa. 51:6)

_____.

H. What attitude will God surely resist in the hearts of His people? (1 Pet. 5:5)

_____.

---

[1] Note that the term *Godhead* is used in Scripture (Romans 1:20).

I. What attitude will God certainly bless in the hearts of His people? (James 4:5)

_____.

J. According to Romans 5:8–9, how was God's love demonstrated to us?

_____.

GOD THE SON–JESUS CHRIST
(CHRISTOLOGY)

I. Instruction: What the Bible teaches us about God the Son

   A. The Deity of Jesus

      1. According to Colossians 2:9, what is said to indwell Jesus Christ in all fullness?

         _____.

      2. What is the Father's specific designation of the Son in Hebrews 1:8?

         _____.

      3. All the angels of God are commanded to do what, regarding the Son? (Heb. 1:6)

         _____.

      4. How long is the Son of God declared to abide, or exist? (Isa. 9:6–7; John 1:1–3, 14; Col. 1:15–17; Heb. 7:3)

         _____.

      5. The Jews sought to destroy Jesus because He made Himself_____ with God. (John 5:18)

      6. In Hebrews 1:3, Jesus Christ is said to be the brightness of God's glory and the express image of whose person?

         _____.

   B. The humanity of Jesus

      1. Jesus was born of a virgin named Mary. How did she conceive without knowing a man? (Matt. 1:20)

         _____.

      2. In taking upon Himself the form of a servant, He was made in the likeness of whom? (Phil. 2:7)

         _____.

3. Jesus was tempted while He was among humanity, but as perfectly and entirely without what? (Heb. 4:15)

_____.

4. Scripture clearly teaches us that Jesus Christ was manifest in the flesh as whom? (John 1:1–3, 14)

_____.

C. The works of Jesus

1. Who made the "worlds" about us, according to Hebrews 1:2?

_____.

2. By whom are all things sustained or "held together" (consist)? (Col. 1:17)

_____.

3. The Bible declares God's Son, Jesus Christ, to be the Savior of what? (John 4:42)

_____.

4. Jesus said that His primary reason for coming into the world was to provide what for many? (Matt. 20:28)

_____.

5. It was the plan of God that Jesus should die on Calvary's cross. His soul was said to be what for the sins of humankind? (Isa. 53:10)

_____.

6. Whose sins did Christ bear on the cross? (1 Pet. 2:24)

_____.

7. Romans 4:25 declares that Jesus was "delivered for our _____ and was raised again for our justification."

8. The bodily resurrection of Jesus from the grave is the basis for what in the believer's life? (1 Cor. 15:19; Tius. 2:13)

_____.

9. In accomplishing the work of redemption, who had power to take Jesus's life from Him and also to raise it up from the grave? (John 10:18)

_____.

10. What is the threefold work of Christ in God's redemptive plan for humankind? (Matt. 21:11) _____, (Heb. 5:5) _____, and (Rev. 19:16) _____.

11. What is Jesus Christ's present ministry at the Father's right hand? (Heb. 4:14)

_____.

12. Jesus is also described as a what, in His present ministry? (1 John 2:1)

_____.

13. Upon His ascension and exaltation, God has set Jesus over the church as her what? (Col. 1:18)

_____.

II. Impact: Application of these truths in my life

A. Because Jesus is the Lord, we are compelled to do what, in relationship to His commandments? (John 14:21)

_____.

B. Since Jesus Christ became flesh and was tempted "in all points life as we are," what may we find from Him that will help us in our time of need? (Heb. 4:16)

_____.

C. What is the atoning blood of Christ able to do for all our sin? (1 John 1:7)

_____.

D. Jesus boldly declared to the scribes at Capernaum that He had "power on earth to forgive" what? (Mark 2:10)

_____.

E. The Apostle Paul describes three distinct aspects of the gospel of Jesus Christ. These three aspects of Christ's saving work are grounded in Scripture prophecy. What are these three aspects we are to believe? (1 Cor. 15:3–4) _____,
_____, and _____.

F. Whom does the Scripture advocate as sole mediator between God and humankind? (1 Tim. 2:5)

_____.

G. Through Christ Jesus, God has purposed that we should have "boldness" and what else, with confidence by faith in Him? (Eph. 3:12)

_____.

H. What other name may we rely upon for our salvation, apart from the Lord Jesus Christ? (Acts 4:12)

_____.

GOD—THE HOLY SPIRIT
(PNEUMATOLOGY)

I. Instruction: What the Bible teaches us about the Holy Spirit

A. The Deity of the Holy Spirit

1. In that Ananias lied against the Holy Spirit (Acts 5:3), to whom did Peter say that Ananias lied as well? (Acts 5:4)

    _____.

2. According to Genesis 1:2, whom does the Bible teach participated in creation?

    _____.

3. The Great Commission of Matthew 28:18–20 bears the authorization of three Persons; who are these Persons? _____, _____, and _____.

4. The psalmist tells us that he could not escape two things pertaining to God. The second is His presence and the first is what? (Psa. 139:7)

    _____.

5. Who has meted out spiritual gifts to the church according to His will? (I Cor. 12:11)

    _____.

6. Believers are charged with the responsibility not to grieve Whom? (Eph. 4:30)

    _____.

7. The eternal existence of God is ascribed specifically to Whom, according to Hebrews 9:14?

    _____.

B. The works of the Holy Spirit

1. Soon after the Holy Spirit created the world, we see Him contending with whom upon the earth? (Gen. 6:3)

    _____.

2. In John 16:8, Jesus said that the Holy Spirit is sent forth from Heaven to reprove the world of three things. What are these three things? _____, _____, and _____.

3. In the Old Testament, whom do we see empowering men for specific tasks and then departing? (Jdg. 3:10; 6:34; 14:6, 19; I Sam. 16:13-14)

   _____.

4. In the New Testament, the Holy Spirit is credited with the virgin birth of whom? (Matt. 1:18) _____.

5. Jesus Christ was filled and led by whom, according to Luke 4:1?

   _____.

6. By what means was Jesus made alive from the dead? (Rom. 8:9-11)

   _____.

7. The work of the Holy Spirit to the Church is extensive. List some of those ministries by writing out the names that are ascribed to Him in the following verses:

   another: _____ (John 14:16)

   Spirit of: _____ (John 14:17)

   Holy Spirit of: _____ (Eph. 1:13)

   Spirit of: _____ (Gal. 4:6)

   Spirit of: _____ (Rom. 8:15)

8. Briefly describe the work of the Holy Spirit, as it is suggested by the following selections of Scripture:

   _____ (Luke 12:12)

   _____ (John 3:6-7; 6:63)

   _____ (John 16:13-14)

   _____ (Eph. 4:30)

   _____ (I Cor. 3:16)

   _____ (Rom. 8:11)

   _____ (Rom. 8:14)

   _____ (Rom. 8:26)

   _____ (I Cor. 12:7 ff.)

II. Impact: The application of these truths to my life

   A. Because the Spirit of God indwells my body, what am I to do in my body, according to First Corinthians 6:20?

      _____.

B. When we choose to surrender our hearts to God as Christians, what is the Holy Spirit able to do within us? (Eph. 5:18)

_____.

C. Jude discusses the need for building up our most holy faith by doing what "in the Holy Spirit"? (v. 20)

_____.

D. List the Spirit fruit that believers are commanded to exhibit in their lives, according to Galatians 5:22-23.

1. _____   6. _____

2. _____   7. _____

3. _____   8. _____

4. _____   9. _____

5. _____

E. If by faith in Christ we live in the realm of the Holy Spirit, the writer of Galatians tells us we must also do what "in the Spirit"? (Gal. 5:25)

_____.

F. According to Second Corinthians 3:17, where the spirit of the Lord reigns, there is assurance of what?

_____.

SATAN—THE ENEMY OF GOD

I. Instruction: What the Bible teaches us about Satan

    A. The existence of Satan

        1. In Matthew 13:39, Jesus refers both to angels and to whom?

            _____.

        2. Whom did Jesus say He personally beheld, or saw, falling from heaven? (Luke 10:18)

            _____.

        3. Whom did Jesus say was a murderer from the beginning? (John 8:44)

            _____.

        4. According to Isaiah 14:13, Lucifer desired to exalt his throne above whom?

            _____.

        5. Jesus declared in Matthew 25:41 that the everlasting fire was prepared for whom?

            _____ and _____.

        6. Ezekiel described Satan as a beautiful, created being before his fall. He is also identified with the highest order of angels. What was his specific rank among the angels, as found in Ezekiel 28:14?

            _____.

    B. The names and nature of Satan

        1. List the names or descriptive titles that are given to Satan from the following verses:

            _____ (I Thess. 3:5)

            _____ (John 12:31)

            _____ (II Cor. 4:4)

            _____ (Eph. 2:2)

            _____ (John 8:44)

            _____ (I John 3:8)

_____ (II Cor. 11:14)

_____ (Rev. 12:10)

_____ (Matt. 12:24)

_____ (II Cor. 6:15)

_____ (Rev. 12:9)

_____ (Rev. 12:3)

_____ (I Pet. 5:8)

2. Job tells us that Satan is a creature with limitations. Who limits the Devil's activity? (Job 1:12)

    _____.

3. Through submission to God, who has the ability to resist Satanic attack? (Jas. 4:7)

    _____.

4. Satan is a doomed creature whose ultimate punishment is what, and for how long? (Rev. 20:10)

    _____.

II. II. Impact: The application of these truths in my life

A. In Second Corinthians 2:11, Paul says that believers are not to be what, concerning Satan's devices?

    _____.

B. According to Ephesians 6:11, what is the Christian's best defense against Satan's wiles (strategy)?

    _____.

C. How is Satan to be resisted by believers? (I Pet. 5:9)

    _____.

D. Through personal submission and yieldedness to God, what will happen to Satan when he is resisted in this manner? (Jas. 4:7)

    _____.

E. What was our Lord's primary resource of defense when He was tempted by the Devil? (Luke 4:4, 8, 12)

    _____.

GOD'S CREATION—MAN'S BEGINNING
(ANTHROPOLOGY)

I. Instruction: What the Bible teaches us about creation and humanity

    A. The creation of the universe

        1. Whom does the Bible declare created the universe all about us? (Gen. 1:1; Neh. 9:6)

            _____.

        2. According to Genesis 1:31, how long did it take God to complete His creative work?

            _____.

        3. Genesis teaches us that a typical creation day consisted of both the evening and the what? (Gen. 1:5, 8, 13, ff.)

            _____.

        4. Hebrews 11:3 tells us that the worlds were framed by what means?

            _____.

        5. The visible universe was not made of things which do appear. How are we to understand this truth biblically? (Heb. 11:3)

            _____.

        6. What two things does creation clearly reveal about God, thus leaving humankind without excuse? (Rom. 1:20) _____ and _____.

    B. The creation of man

        1. Once God formed man from the dust of the ground, breathed into his nostrils the breath of life, what did man become? (Gen. 2:7)

            _____.

         2. Scripture tells us that mankind was made a reflection of his Creator in two specific ways. What are these two reflecting qualities? (Gen. 1:26-27)

            _____ and _____.

3. Man (Adam) was created a morally responsible being, in that God gave him charge of what? (Gen. 2:15)

   _____.

4. Adam's keen intellect becomes evident when he identifies and names what three groups of living things? (Gen. 2:20) _____,

   _____, and _____.

5. What was God's purpose for creating humanity and the universe about us? (Rev. 4:11)

   _____.

6. To provide companionship and support for Adam, whom did God create from man's own flesh? (Gen. 2:23)

   _____.

7. Our first parents were created in perfect innocence, seeing that they were both naked and were not what? (Gen. 2:25)

   _____.

8. Mankind was created with the ability to choose between right and wrong. The consequence of his own choice to violate the commandment of God would result in what? (Gen. 2:16-17)

   _____.

9. Briefly relate the temptation and fall of mankind, according to Genesis 3:1-13. Pay careful attention to the nature of Satan's temptation and the self-justifying attempts of man to cover his offense.

   _____

   _____

   _____

   _____

   _____.

10. As the head and progenitor of the human race, Adam's sin brought what upon all humanity? (Rom. 5:12)

    _____.

II. Impact: The application of these truths in my life

   A. In the context of God's work of creation, the Psalmist stirs up his soul to do what? (Psa. 104:1)

      _____.

B. According to Romans 1:25, how does a corrupt heart turn the truth of God into a lie?

_____.

C. Although Adam brought the peril of sin upon the human race, how many are likewise found guilty of deliberate sin against God's nature? (Rom. 3:23)

_____.

D. Upon being found guilty in the sight of God, what provision did God make for the consciousness of shame that Adam and Eve felt? (Gen. 3:21)

_____.

E. Among the many consequences of man's sin against the Lord, what specific emotional response from Adam do we clearly notice in Genesis 3:10?

_____.

F. Who alone could provide the remedy for mankind's fear and shame, according to Genesis 3:21 and Acts 4:12?

_____.

SIN—MORAL WRONG

(HAMARTIOLOGY)

I. Instruction: What the Bible teaches us about sin

A. Sin defined

1. The Bible clearly identifies the nature and essence of sin. With one word, describe sin as it appears in the Scripture verses below. Sin is what?

_____ First John 5:17

_____ Romans 14:23

_____ Isaiah 59:2

_____ Genesis 39:9

_____ Jeremiah 17:9

_____ First John 3:4

In brief, sin is anything, whether done willfully or in ignorance, against the will and character of God.

B. Sin's origin

1. In whom does the Bible tell us that sin was first found? (Isa. 14:12-14; Ezk. 28:14-15)

_____.

2. How did sin first enter the human race? (Rom. 5:12)

_____.

3. According to the Bible, sin penetrates every aspect of a person's nature from birth. What two specific things does Solomon conclude concerning the human heart? (Ecc. 9:3) It is _____

and _____.

4. When does sin first infect each member of Adam's offspring? (Psa. 51:5; Eph. 2:3)

_____.

C. Sin's consequences

1. The sin problem has infected how many human beings? (Rom. 3:23)

   _____.

2. The just penalty for sin, deserved by every member of the human race, is what? (Rom. 6:23)

   _____.

3. God's ultimate judgment for sin is the second death. What is the second death? (Rev. 20:13-15)

   _____.

4. Apart from spiritual death, what was the inevitable consequence of a person's physical life, as a result of sin? (Gen. 2:17; Rom. 6:23)

   _____.

5. What are some of the physical consequences of sin, as seen in Genesis 3:16-19?

   _____.

   _____.

   _____.

   _____.

   _____.

6. Sin is responsible for humanity's moral and mental deterioration. Identify some of sin's poisonous fruit from Romans 1:21-32 and Galatians 5:19-21.

   _____   _____

   _____   _____

   _____   _____

   _____   _____

   _____   _____

7. The Bible declares but one means whereby condemned sinners may escape the just desserts of their sin. What is that means? (Rom. 5:6-11)

   _____.

II. Impact: The application of these truths in my life

   A. In our natural state, apart from the grace of God, what things are we unable to receive? (I Cor. 2:14)

   _____.

B. Apart from the salvation that God offers man through Christ Jesus, what is a realistic view of our spiritual condition before the Holy God? (Eph. 2:1)

_____.

C. Because man's nature is completely under sin's reign, even our righteous moral works are as what? (Isa. 64:6)

_____.

D. Without the deliverance that Christ provides, how many of us understand God and seek Him the right way? (Rom. 3:11)

_____.

E. Seeing that the quality of the human heart is depraved, what must God do for us, which no one can do for their selves? (Eph. 2:1; Titus 3:5)

_____.

F. How is the imputed righteousness of God known to the heart of a condemned sinner? (Rom. 3:22)

_____.

G. It is the nature of sin to make everyone subject to what, all of his life? (Heb. 2:15)

_____.

H. It is the nature of God's truth to make everyone what? (John 8:32)

_____.

There is no bondage of sin that God's grace cannot liberate in the lives of humankind!

SALVATION–SPIRITUAL DELIVERANCE
(SOTERIOLOGY)

I. Instruction: What the Bible teaches us about God's salvation

  A. Salvation defined

    1. The word "salvation" means deliverance. John 3:16 declares that through faith in Jesus Christ, the believer is delivered from what?

    _____.

    2. How else are we told that individuals are delivered by God, according to Hebrews 2:15?

    _____.

  God's salvation is two-fold. It entails deliverance from both sin's penalty of eternal punishment and sin's power in our daily lives.

    3. Salvation is described in Scripture as whose work? (Eph. 2:8-9)

    _____.

  B. The basis for salvation

    1. Salvation is only possible through whom? (Rom. 5:8-11)

    _____.

    2. What is the means God has chosen to reconcile lost people (the enemies of God) to Himself? (Rom. 5:10)

    _____.

    3. Unless Christ was raised from the grave, what effect would His death have upon our sin? (I Cor. 15:17)

    _____.

    4. The benefit of God's salvation is wholly and solely a provision of God's what? (Eph. 2:8-9)

    _____.

5. How is the saving work of Jesus Christ appropriated to one's life? (John 1:12)

_____.

6. What is the basis for God's legal justification of the sinner? (Rom. 3:26)

_____.

7. What part do good works or human effort play in receiving God's salvation? (Rom. 3:28; Eph. 2:8-9)

_____.

8. Even the element of belief does not merit salvation, for the Bible tells us that we are justified by what? (Titus 3:7)

_____.

C. Elements of personal salvation

1. List some of the personal blessings of trusting Christ for salvation:

_____ First Peter 1:3-4

_____ Romans 3:25

_____ Ephesians 1:6

_____ Ephesians 2:19

_____ Galatians 4:5

_____ Galatians 2:20

_____ Romans 3:24

_____ Philippians 3:20

_____ Second Corinthians 5:17

_____ Romans 6:14

2. The Bible tells us that the believer in Christ Jesus was chosen "in Him" at what time? (Eph. 1:4)

_____.

3. The good work of grace, which God began in the sinner's heart at conversion, will continue how long? (Phiip. 1:6)

_____.

4. God's ultimate purpose in the salvation of lost sinners is to bring them into conformity to what? (Rom. 8:29)

_____.

II. Impact: The application of these truths in my life

    A. Before we can understand our need for Jesus Christ, how are we to see ourselves before the Holy God? (Isa. 53:6; Rom. 5:8)

    _____.

    _____.

    B. Without God's salvation, what is our real prospect for the future? (Eph. 2:12)

    _____.

    _____.

    C. What practical effects does God's saving grace have upon our living in "this present world"? (Titus 2:11-12)

    _____.

    _____.

    _____.

    D. What does God's grace ordain in the believer's life once Christ is trusted for salvation? (Eph. 2:10)

    _____.

    E. What two things describe our attitude toward the continuance of good works, once we become Christians? (Philp. 2:12-13) _____ and _____.

    F. Becoming a believer in Christ Jesus involves obedience to the Gospel (doctrine) from what? (Rom. 6:17)

    _____.

    G. Paul describes God's work of grace in the life of a sinner as a turning from something and a turning unto something. What are these two contrasting elements? (I Thess. 1:9) From _____ to _____.

III. Invitation: God's offer of salvation to you

    1. Who makes this offer? (Rom. 5:8)

    _____.

    2. Why do you need it? (Rom. 3:23; 6:23)

    _____.

    3. What is eternal life? (John 17:3)

    _____.

    4. What did it cost God to provide salvation for you? (I Pet. 1:18-19)

    _____.

5. What will it cost you to receive it? (Rom. 6:23)

    _____.

6. How do you receive it? (John 1:12; 3:16)

    _____.

7. Why does God make you such an offer? (I John 4:9)

    _____.

8. What is the guarantee? (John 10:28)

    _____.

9. When must you decide? (II Cor. 6:2)

    _____.

10. Where can you find out more about this offer? (Rom. 10:17)

    _____.

THE CHURCH—MYSTERY OF GRACE

(ECCLESIOLOGY)

I. Instruction: What the Bible teaches us about the church

   A. The church at large identified

      1. The church of Jesus Christ began on what day, according to the book of Acts? (Acts 2:1)

         _____.

      2. Who is responsible for placing (baptizing) believers into the body of Christ, the church? (I Cor. 12:13)

         _____.

      3. Until Christ returns to take His church away from this world, who are those who make up this great flock? (Acts 2:41; Rom. 8:9; I Cor. 12:13)

         _____.

      4. Who is the only righteous Head of the church? (Col. 1:18)

         _____.

   B. The local church identified

      1. What two things characterized the individuals who were first added to the Jerusalem church? (Acts 2:41) _____
         and _____.

         Although baptism is not a biblical requirement for salvation or for entrance into Christ's body at large, it nonetheless becomes a credible confession of faith for local church membership.

      2. What four activities do we see the believers doing in the Jerusalem assembly? (Acts 2:42)

         _____   _____

         _____   _____

         In earliest of times and as the situation calls for the need, local churches have met where? (Rom. 16:5) _____.

3. List the seven local churches of Asia Minor that are recorded in Revelation 2 and 3:

_____   _____

_____   _____

_____   _____

_____

C. Offices and ordinances of the church

1. What two positions of leadership has God ordained for the local church? (I Tim. 3:1, 8) _____ and _____.

2. According to Acts 6:2-3, which position of the local church was first elected to tend to the temporal needs of the church?

_____.

3. In Acts 20:28, the pastors are commended by Paul to occupy themselves in doing what to the "church of God"?

_____.

4. What ordinance, which Jesus established, was practiced and perpetuated by the early church? (Acts 2:42; I Cor. 11:26) _____

_____.

5. What ordinance do we observe being practiced by the early church on the day of Pentecost? (Acts 2:41)

_____.

6. Summarize the biblical mandate of Jesus Christ from Matthew 28:19-20. Discuss how this Great Commission involves the church today. _____

_____

_____

_____

_____.

D. The purpose of the church

1. What does God purpose that the church should demonstrate before the world, according to First Peter 2:9? _____

_____.

2. God would have His people do good to whom? (Gal. 6:10) _____

_____.

3. Believers have a special ministry obligation to whom? (Gal. 6:10; Heb. 10:24)

_____.

4. In order for the church to reproduce holy Christians, what must every Christian seek to do? (II Tim. 2:2) _____

_____.

II. Impact: The application of these truths in my life

A. Because the local church is God's plan for His people, what are we never to forsake? (Heb. 10:25)

_____.

B. A Christian should provide his or her service to the church for its increase and what? (Eph. 4:16)

_____.

C. What should be our relationship, as believers, to biblically qualified pastors (Heb. 13:17)

_____.

D. What is our responsibility before God, upon hearing pastoral admonition? (Acts 17:11)

_____.

E. The practical and logistical ministry and business of the church should be the primary concern of _____? (Acts 6:3, 5)

F. The strategic and spiritual ministry and business of the church should be the primary concern of _____? (Acts 20:17, 28; Titus 1:5)

G. List those spiritual qualifications of church leadership that all of us should seek to model, according to First Timothy 3:1-10.

LAST THINGS

(ESCHATOLOGY)

I. Instruction: What the Bible teaches us about last things

A. Christ's return for His church

1. Jesus promised His disciples that one day He would return to do what to the living saints who are upon the earth? (John 14:3)

   _____.

2. Before Jesus returns to establish His earthly Kingdom, where does He first take believers who are living on the earth when He comes again? (I Thess. 4:17)

   _____.

3. In the context of the return of Jesus and coming judgment upon the earth, what did Paul tell believers that God had not appointed for them? (I Thess. 5:9)

   _____.

4. After describing the Laodicean church attitude and era, what did the apostle John hear the trumpet saying in Revelation 4:1?

   _____.

B. Tribulation upon the earth

1. The book of the Revelation speaks largely of a time of judgment of sin upon this world. What does Matthew 24:21 call this period of God's wrath?

   _____.

2. Who will be a leading figure, opposing God Himself, during this period of divine judgment? (II Thess. 2:3, 8)

   _____.

3. What event of Bible prophecy will mark an end to the anti-Christ forces and the tribulation hour? (Matt. 24:29-31)

   _____.

C. Christ's earthly millennium

1. After the Lord judges sin upon this world, how long will His reign continue upon the earth? (Rev. 20:4-7)

_____.

2. In what spirit will Jesus Christ rule His Kingdom upon the earth? (Isa. 11:2)

_____   _____

_____   _____

_____   _____

_____   _____

3. What will be the Capital of Christ's coming kingdom? (Isa. 2:3)

_____.

4. The establishment of an earthly kingdom by Jesus Christ fulfills God's promise and prophesy that He made to two Old Testament personalities. Who are they? (Gen. 15:18; II Sam. 7:16) _____ and _____.

D. The Final Judgment

The Bible teaches that Satan, who is bound for the duration of the millennium, will be loosed at the end of the 1,000 years, in order to deceive the nations (Rev. 20:7-8). His uprising will be short, and God shall cast him, at last and finally, into the lake of fire (Rev. 20:10).

1. What type of throne is depicted as the place of final judgment for all unbelieving men and women? (Rev. 20:11)

_____.

2. Whom did the Apostle John see standing before God at the judgment? (Rev. 20:12)

_____.

3. Who is ultimately condemned to the lake of fire, according to Revelation 20:15?

_____.

4. Certainly, the unrighteous works of the unbelieving give witness to the unbelief of the dead (Rev. 20:12). Who directly examines the life record of the dead, according to Revelation 20:12?

_____.

E. The reality of heaven and hell

1. According to Isaiah 66:1, what is heaven? _____

_____.

2. Jesus speaks of heaven as His Father's what? (John 14:2) _____

   _____.

3. John 14:3 designates heaven as a particular what? _____

   _____.

4. Who are the occupants of heaven's fair city? (Rev. 22:8-9, 14) _____

   _____.

5. How long will heaven, its subjects, and its blessings last? (Rev. 22:5) _____

   _____.

6. Hell appears to be the temporal holding place of the unbelieving dead. Where is hell
   finally cast? (Rev. 20:14) _____

   _____.

7. Hell and the lake of fire both have something which cannot be quenched. What is
   this thing? (Mark 9:43-44) _____

   _____.

8. What effect did the flame have upon the rich man in the Biblical account of Lazarus?
   (Luke 16:24)_____

   _____.

9. Who are the recipients of eternal punishment and ruin?

   _____ John 3:18

   _____ Matthew 25:41

   _____ Revelation 20:10

   _____ Matthew 7:23

   _____ Second Thessalonians 2:12

   _____ John 3:36

10. What New Testament personality spoke most about hell and did the most to keep
    people from it?

    _____.

II. Impact: The application of these truths in my life

   A. In view of the coming judgment of Christ, what two things does Peter tell us should
      characterize our manner of living? (II Pet. 3:11) _____
      and _____.

B. What effect does the truth of our Lord's return have upon Christians who are bereaved of believing loved ones? (I Thess. 4:13, 18) _____

_____.

C. As believers, we are compelled to live responsibly, seeing we must appear before whom? (II Cor. 5:10)

_____.

D. In what perspective are we, as Christians, to labor in this present world? (II Cor. 5:9)

_____.

E. The Bible never gives us the specific date for Christ's return for His own. How is the Lord's coming described in First Thessalonians 5:2?

_____.

F. What practical impact should the imminence of Christ's return have upon our lives? (I Thess. 5:6)

_____.

G. Knowledge of the great exhibition of God's wrath upon sin and unrighteousness compels us to what action, regarding all men? (II Cor. 5:11)

_____.

H. Angels will once again play a visible and strategic role in the completion of end-time prophecy. How should believers continually perceive these elect supernatural beings? (Rev. 22:8-9)

_____.

I. In Titus 2:13, what terms does Paul use to describe the glorious appearing of Jesus Christ?

_____.

SANCTIFICATION–
THE BELIEVER'S WALK

I. Instruction: What the Bible teaches us about living

A. Sanctification explained

1. The word "sanctification" is used in a two-fold way. It first involves an initial and positional separation unto God in holiness and, secondly, a progressive and practical separation from evil in a believer's life. According to First Thessalonians 4:3, the sanctification of the believer is said to be the will of whom?

    _____.

2. Sanctification is both positional and progressive. On the one hand, the believer is entirely sanctified before God through the sacrifice of Christ (Heb. 10:10); on the other hand, the believer is admonished to sanctify the Lord in what place? (I Pet. 3:15)

    _____.

3. God intends to sanctify His own people through the use of what means? (John 17:17)

    _____.

4. What other Agent is involved in the sanctification of the believer? (Rom. 15:16)

    _____.

5. By His death, it was the purpose of Jesus Christ to do what two things to the people He came to redeem? (Eph. 5:25-26) _____
    and _____.

B. Sanctification exhibited

1. The believer exhibits sanctification by what he says!

    a. In contrast to the corrupt communication that characterizes the ungodly world, the believer's tongue is to minister what to others? (Eph. 4:29)

        _____.

b. What is the first way Timothy could be an example of sanctity to other Christians, according to First Timothy 4:12?

_____.

c. What is the nature of the speech that cannot be condemned? (Titus 2:8)

_____.

d. In word, as well as deed, Christians are to do all in the name of whom? (Col. 3:17)

_____.

e. By what two ways does the believer exercise sanctity in his speech? (I Pet. 3:10)

_____ and _____.

f. List those particular manifestations of the tongue which believers are to put off, according to Colossians 3:8-9.

_____   _____

_____   _____

_____   _____

g. According to Colossians 3:16, in what manner does the sanctified tongue find its expression?

_____   _____

_____   _____

_____   _____

2. The believer exhibits sanctification by what he does!
   a. Sanctity in the Christian life is evident when Christians separate themselves from practices like those of Colossians 3:5. List these six practices:

   _____   _____

   _____   _____

   _____   _____

   b. How should every Christian possess his vessel (body), according to First Thessalonians 4:4?

   _____ and _____.

   c. In First Thessalonians 4:3, Paul specifically states that sanctification involves abstinence from what?

   _____.

   d. Sanctification, furthermore, involves abstinence from the appearance of what? (I Thess. 5:22)

   _____.

   e. In Christ Jesus, believers have become servants to what type of practice, according to Romans 6:19?

_____.

f. What specific thoughts are to be cultivated in the mind which is set apart to holy living? (Philp. 4:8)

_____   _____

_____   _____

_____   _____

g. In First Peter 1:15, the word "conversation" has to do with both word and deed. In what manner is practical sanctification, or personal holiness, to affect the believer's conversation? _____

_____.

3. The believer exhibits sanctification by the attitude he cultivates!

a. The Apostle Paul readily admitted to his imperfection. Paul's frame of mind, however, was to press toward what? (Philp. 3:14)

_____.

b. The Apostle John admonished believers to be perfect in intent when he wrote in First John 2:1 that believers should never do what?

_____.

c. The Psalmist purposed in his mind to "hide God's Word in his heart" for what purpose? (Psa. 119:11)

_____.

d. What is the God-honoring attitude of Christians who face trials and temptations? (I Pet. 1:6)

_____.

e. What attitude will God firmly resist in the life of a believer? (I Pet. 5:5)

_____.

f. What attitude will result in God's increased blessing and strength for Christian living? (Jas. 4:6)

_____.

g. Romans 3:4 relates an attitude of utter confidence in God, by presenting a stark contrast between God and mankind. What is this contrast?

_____.

4. The believer exhibits sanctification by the fellowship he keeps!

a. The Bible commands believers to do what two things, with regard to "unfruitful works of darkness"? (Eph. 5:11) _____

but rather _____.

b. What is the basis of genuine Christian fellowship, according to First John 1:7?

_____.

c. Christians are to refrain from yokes of partnership with what group of people? (II Cor. 6:14) _____.

d. Although Jesus was known as a "friend of publicans and sinners" (Matt. 11:19), He remained, nonetheless, separate from whom? (Heb. 7:26)

_____.

e. List some of the biblical grounds that make it necessary for Christians to separate themselves from another Christian brother, according to First Corinthians 5:11.

_____   _____

_____   _____

_____   _____

_____   _____

f. What is God's admonition to believers, with reference to religious apostates? (Rom. 16:17) _____.

g. Regular fellowship with those of like precious faith is not to be what? (Heb. 10:25) _____.

II. Impact: The application of these truths in my life

A. The ultimate desire of our hearts as Christians should be to do what? (Rom. 15:6)

_____.

B. How can we glorify God as believers? (Psa. 86:12; Rom. 12:1; I Cor. 6:20; 2 Cor. 9:13; Col. 3:16; 1 Pet. 2:12)

_____.

C. What is the nature and the effect of God's truth upon our lives? (Titus 1:1)

_____.

D. List the two commands for practical sanctification, as Paul gives them to us in Second Corinthians 7:1.

_____.

_____.

E. When will our practical sanctification be completed? (I John 3:2)

_____.

F. Who is unfailing to help us in the process of personal holiness and practical sanctification? (I Thess. 5:23)

_____.

G. Upon what grounds does the Apostle Paul beseech us as Christians to be living sacrifices? (Rom. 12:1)

_____.

H. As children of light, we are to pursue two primary objectives in this world of darkness. What are these two things? (Matt. 6:33) _____

and _____.

I. Besides bringing glory to Himself, what impact does the Lord intend our lives to have upon an on looking world? (Matt. 5:16) _____

_____.

THREE HELPS FOR OVERCOMING
SIN AND SERIOUS DIFFICULTY

I. Instruction: What the Bible teaches us about change

   A. Repentance: Identifying sin and forsaking it

      1. Jesus taught that genuine repentance results in "bringing forth" what? (Matt. 3:8)

         _____.

      2. What is the fruit that is manifested in believers' lives, when they turn away from their sin? (Rom. 6:22; Gal. 5:22-23)

         _____.

      3. Biblical change is possible in the life of the Christian, since sin may no longer exercise what over the child of God? (Rom. 6:14)

         _____.

      4. The admonition of Paul in Romans 6:12 is that believers should not allow sin to do what in their bodies?

         _____.

      5. Before repentance can be truly enjoined, the Christian must come to terms with sin through what means? (I John 1:9)

         _____.

   B. Rehabituation: Replacing sinful patterns with righteous habits

      1. What does the Holy Spirit tell believers to "put off" in Ephesians 4:22?

         _____.

      2. What does the Holy Spirit tell believers to "put on" in Ephesians 4:24?

         _____.

3. In First Timothy 4:7, Paul sets forth a dynamic principle for growth in the Christian life when he instructs Timothy to practice what?

_____.

4. Through what means do the senses become equipped to discern "both good and evil"? (Heb. 5:14)

_____.

5. The difficulty Israel faced in breaking her rebellious pattern was largely due to her long habit of doing what? (Jer. 13:23)

_____.

C. Resources: Biblical helps for effecting change

1. A primary resource that God has given believers, enabling them to effectively deal with their sin struggles, is what? (John 17:17)

_____.

2. Another resource that requires diligent use in the believer's life is what? (I Thess. 5:17)

_____.

3. According to Hebrews 10:25, the cultivation of which resource is remedial to the Christian's spiritual perspective and performance?

_____.

4. What is the divine, essential resource and dynamic of the Christian life, without which we are doomed to defeat? (John 16:13-14)

_____.

II. Impact: The application of these truths to my life

A. In making the break from sinful habits, what do we need to know about our flesh? (Rom. 6:6)

_____.

B. What are we to reckon in our lives, according to Romans 6:11?

_____.

C. In Christ Jesus, we are now freed to yield our physical members as instruments of what? (Rom. 6:13)

_____.

D. List the contrasting works and fruits that are mentioned in Galatians 5:19-23.

WORKS TO BE PUT OFF   FRUIT TO BE PUT ON

_____   _____

_____   _____

_____   _____

_____   _____

_____   _____

_____   _____

_____   _____

_____   _____

_____   _____

_____   _____

E. What is God's promise to each of us who pursues God in diligence? (Heb. 11:6)

_____.

HELPS FOR UNDERSTANDING
YOUR BIBLE

I. Basic overview of the Bible

A. The Old Testament

1. The Law, or The Pentateuch: Genesis to Deuteronomy
    The writings of Moses, which include the account of creation, the fall of mankind, the called-out people of God, the wilderness wanderings, and the death of Moses.

2. The Writings: Joshua to Song of Solomon
    A large collection of Jewish writings which include the rise and fall of God's people in the land of promise, stories and records of God's providential dealings with the Jewish people, wise counsel from God-fearing men, and commentaries on suffering, praise, perspective, and noted proverbs.

3. The Prophets: Isaiah to Malachi
    Larger and smaller prophetic books that speak of God's mercy and justice upon a rebellious people; the utterances are filled with messianic hope and future predictions of God's sovereign movement throughout Jewish and world history.

B. The New Testament

1. The Doings and Sayings of Jesus: Matthew to John
    The record of the Gospels is the record of the life and times of Jesus Christ. The teachings of Christ permeate the Gospels, with the eyewitness development of the Lord's walk among humanity.

2. The Documents and Doctrines of the Church: Acts to Jude
    The book of Acts is basically an inspired history of the spread of Christianity and the growth of the early church. The rest of the books within this category provide us with the primary doctrine of the Christian Church. The apostolic literature covers a broad range of study and represents the official teaching of the true Church of Jesus Christ.

3. <u>The Dominion of Jesus Christ</u>: Revelation

The book of the Revelation sets forth prophetic details that concern end-times, as well as the conclusion of world history. It is the book of Christ's ultimate conquest of all His enemies and the establishment of God's eternal Day.

II. Basic Rules of Bible Study

A. Always approach your Bible as a prayerful hearer. Seek to make ready application of God's truth to your own life (Ezra 7:10).

B. Read the entire context of the verses you are studying. Ask the basic questions: who, what, when, where, why, how?

C. Recreate the atmosphere, attitude, motives, and emotions of the writer in your own mind. Interpret the text in his mindset, not your own.

D. Assimilate the truth you have learned to your own heart and life. Look for God in the sacred pages and turn what you learn about Him into knowledge of Him!

III. Basic Bible Study Tools

A. Bible concordance: "An alphabetical index of words in a book … with the passages in which they occur" (Webster).
*Reputable one-volume concordances:

1. *Strong's Exhaustive Concordance of the Bible*

2. *Young's Analytical Concordance of the Bible*

3. *Zondervan's Expanded Concordance*

B. Bible commentary: written findings, conclusions, interpretations, and evaluations of others' understanding of the Christian Scriptures.
*Reputable one-volume commentaries:

1. *Zondervan's Matthew Henry Bible Commentary*

2. *Zondervan's Commentary on the Whole Bible*

C. Bible dictionary: a dictionary that will inform the reader as to the meaning of biblical terminology, i.e., "Pharisee."
*Reputable one-volume dictionaries:

1. *Zondervan's Pictorial Bible Dictionary*

2. *Tenney's Handy Dictionary of the Bible*

D. Bible handbook: a study tool that will inform you as to the sense and meaning of Scripture from an historical, archaeological, and encyclopedic approach.

*Reputable one-volume handbooks:

1. *Unger's Bible Handbook*

2. *Halley's Bible Handbook*

HELPS FOR MAINTAINING PRIVATE DEVOTIONS

Meaning: Maintaining private or personal devotions has to do with the cultivation, by the means of personal prayer and Bible study, of increased love and loyalty to God.

I.   The need for personal devotion

    A.   Apparent from biblical commands: Colossians 3:16; Second Timothy 2:15; Second Peter 3:18

    B.   Apparent from biblical illustrations: Enoch in Genesis 5:22, Isaac in Genesis 24:63, Joshua in Joshua 1:8, David in Psalm 119:2, and Jesus in Mark 1:35.

II. The time of personal devotions
Scripture does not specify an exact time for personal devotions, only that both day and night are seasonable for meditation.

    A.   The Psalmist said, "Early will I seek Thee" (Psa. 63:1; note: "early" may express urgency).

    B.   Isaac "went into the fields at eventide to meditate" (Gen. 24:63).

    C.   Godly believers, such as Spurgeon, Edwards, Hamm, and Mueller, would not so much as begin a day's activities without spending sufficient time with the Master.
The important thing to remember about devotions is that it must be a time of solitude, when the door of care is shut; it is a time long enough to leave His sweet fragrance upon our hearts throughout our daily activity.

III. The objectives of personal devotions

    A.   To increase our love for Christ: if our private devotions do not result in this, then we are going through a mere mechanical exercise!

    B.   To know Christ's leading (Psa. 119:105)

    C.   To rise above temptation (Psa. 119:11)

    D.   To grow in grace through spiritual exercise (I Tim. 4:8, 15)

CONCLUSION

Practice makes perfect; likewise, the Christian's spiritual maturity rises only to the extent that he has been exercised in God's Word (I Tim. 4:7).

Printed in the United States
by Baker & Taylor Publisher Services